D0931723

The Good Samaritan
and other stories

Peter Watkins & Erica Hughes

The Good Samaritan and other stories

Illustrated by Nigel Murray

Julia MacRae Books
A division of Franklin Watts

Text © 1987 Peter Watkins and Erica Hughes
Illustrations © 1987 Nigel Murray
All rights reserved
First published in Great Britain 1987 by
Julia MacRae Books
A division of Franklin Watts
12a Golden Square, London, W1R 4BA
and Franklin Watts, Australia
14 Mars Road, Lane Cove, NSW 2066

Watkins, Peter, 1934–
    The good samaritan and other stories. —
    (Redwing series).
    1. Jesus Christ — Parables — Juvenile
    literature   2. Bible stories, English –
    N.T.
    I. Title   II. Hughes, Erica
    226'.809505   BT376
ISBN 0–86203–255–5

Phototypeset by Ace Filmsetting Ltd, Frome, Somerset
Printed and bound in Great Britain by
Adlard & Son Ltd.
The Garden City Press, Letchworth

Contents

To Celia Jordan

Parables are stories with a difference. On the surface they are very simple and easy to understand, but on a deeper level they are 'tales of the unexpected'. They are told, not just for enjoyment and interest, but principally to make the listener sit up and take notice, and then question the way he has so far lived his life.

Parable *comes from a Greek word meaning 'comparison'. Like other Jewish rabbis, or teachers, Jesus taught much of the time in parables; He told stories which dealt with the ordinary things of everyday life. His listeners understood about farmers in fields, shepherds with their flocks, and travellers with business to transact. Jesus used these familiar subjects to illustrate a particular truth which he wanted to emphasise. You could say that his parables are 'earthly' stories with a 'heavenly' meaning.*

For two thousand years these stories have influenced people's lives. Phrases from them are built into our language: expressions like 'passing by on the other side' and 'safe and sound' come from versions of the parables of Jesus.

Perhaps the best way of showing what makes these parables such very special stories is by telling yet another story.

A rabbi was once asked why he told so many stories. He answered:

"There was a time when Truth went around naked and unadorned, and whoever saw Truth turned away, in fear or shame, and gave him no welcome. So Truth wandered through the lands of the earth, rebuffed and unwanted.

"One day, feeling disconsolate, he met Parable, strolling along happily in smart and bright clothes. 'Truth, why are you so sad?' asked Parable cheerfully. 'Because I am so old and so ugly that everyone avoids me,' answered Truth. 'Nonsense,' said Parable. 'That is not why people avoid you. Here – borrow some of my clothes and see what happens.'

"And so Truth put on some of Parable's clothes and everywhere he went he was welcomed."

The rabbi smiled and said: "The truth is that men cannot face the naked Truth; they much prefer him disguised."

1 The Good Samaritan

A man who lived in the city of Jerusalem set out one day on a journey. With his pack on his back, he walked out of the city gates and took the long hilly road down to Jericho. He knew it would take him some hours, perhaps all day, to get there so he made an early start.

At first the road stretched smoothly ahead and the traveller made good progress. But as he left the city further and further behind, he found that the going got harder. The road twisted and turned round the mountainside. The surface was rough and rocky, and here and there great boulders were dotted around. I must be careful here, thought the traveller. Besides the danger of falling down on this rough pathway, there is also the risk of being robbed.

I have heard of people travelling alone like myself, being set on by robbers in these parts.

He tried to hurry his footsteps but almost at once his worst fears were realised. As he rounded a bend, a band of men suddenly sprang out from behind the rocks and knocked him to the ground. He fought back bravely but

he was only one against many. They seized his baggage, stripped him of his clothes, then beat him up and left him lying half dead by the side of the road. As he lay there, battered and bleeding and quite unable to drag himself out of the glare of the midday sun, he knew that his only hope was that some other traveller might be using the road and would come to his rescue.

At last someone came by. He was a priest from the great Temple in Jerusalem, but when he saw the figure huddled by the roadside he thought only of his own safety. "That man has been attacked," he said to himself. "Perhaps the robbers are still around." So he quickened his pace and kept as far away as he could on the other side of the road.

Not long afterwards, following in his footsteps, came another man. He was also from Jerusalem, a priest's special assistant called a Levite. When he caught sight of the wounded man, he too looked nervously over his shoulder and hurried on.

After the priest and the Levite had gone on their selfish ways, the road remained empty and silent for some time. Then came the clip-clopping sound of a donkey's hooves and along came a traveller from a distant part of the country called Samaria. Priests and Levites were respected and respectable people, but Samaritans were a despised race.

When the Samaritan saw the injured man, he dismounted and went over to him at once. Poor fellow, he is badly hurt, he thought. I don't know where he comes from – he doesn't look like one of my countrymen. But he needs help. I must look after him.

So he bathed his wounds with wine to cleanse and disinfect them, and with oil to soothe and heal them. He gave him water to drink from his flask, wrapped him in his cloak, and then lifted him carefully on to his donkey's back. "He is in no fit state to be left," he said to himself. "I had better take him back to that inn I passed on the way and see if we can stay there for the night."

It was a painful, jolting journey but the Samaritan led him as slowly and gently as he could, never thinking for a moment of the possible dangers to himself. When they eventually reached the inn, the inn-keeper showed them to a room. All night the good Samaritan watched over his patient, bathing his poor bruised body and feeding him with little sips of water and wine. He looked after the stranger as carefully as if he were his next door neighbour.

In the morning the Samaritan gave the inn-keeper two silver coins.

"I cannot stay any longer," he said. "I must continue on my way. Please take care of him. Get him anything he needs, and when I come back I will repay you whatever you have spent on him."

The grateful invalid, when left alone, certainly had something to think about. "All my life," he said to himself, "I have looked up to priests and Levites. But when I really needed help it was a Samaritan who acted towards me like a good neighbour should."

2 The Lost Sheep

There was once a shepherd who had to take care of a flock of a hundred sheep. Every morning he led them out into the pasture, and every evening he led them back to the sheepfold and shut them up safely for the night, counting them first to make sure they were all there. He knew them all so well that he could give each sheep a name, and they knew his voice so well that they would come at once when they heard him call.

Early one morning, when the sun had just risen, the shepherd got up as usual. He wrapped his cloak round his shoulders and picked up his curved shepherd's crook. Then he opened the gate of the sheepfold and called to the sheep and lambs asleep inside. Out they all streamed

and soon the air was filled with bleating and
baaing as they followed the shepherd along the
stony track which led up to the lower slopes of
the mountain. Here the early morning dew still
lay on the grass, the sun was casting long
shadows, and the air was sweet with the scent
of wild flowers.

All day the shepherd sat under a tree
watching as his flock contentedly nibbled the
juicy grass. He knew he must not take his eyes
off them, for, although the place looked peaceful
and pleasant, wolves roamed the countryside
and at any time one might creep out from
behind a rock and snatch a young lamb.

There was one young sheep that day that was
restless. It tried first one clump of grass and

16

then another, until gradually it had moved further and further away from all the other sheep. The grass higher up the slopes looked temptingly green and lush, so at last the foolish sheep left the rest of the flock and went off on its own.

When the sun began to set, the shepherd knew it was time to gather the sheep together and take them home. Obediently they came to his call, clustering round him and following him back down the mountainside. But the foolish sheep had strayed too far to hear his voice and it was not with the others.

As they entered the sheepfold, the shepherd leaned on his crook and counted the sheep as he always did: "... ninety-seven, ninety-eight, ninety-nine ... I should have a hundred sheep," he said, "and I have counted only ninety-nine. One of them is missing."

He called softly, then more and more loudly, but the little sheep was too far away to hear his call.

Then the weary shepherd realised that one of his beloved sheep was lost. There was only one thing to do; he must go back up the darkening mountainside and look for it. Having made sure that the other ninety-nine were safely settled, he picked up his lantern and started off along the road. The way back seemed very long, for the shepherd was tired and he was hungry for his supper.

It grew darker and the shepherd found it harder and harder to find his way. But all he

could think about was his lost sheep. As he
trudged along he kept calling to it, but still
there was no answer. The way became steeper
and rougher, until at last he had climbed as
high as he could go. This was a dangerous place
where wild animals had their lairs among the
rocks. He called once more, and, as he listened,
he heard a faint bleating sound coming from a

crevice. Lifting up his lantern he saw, cowering
in the shadows, the frightened, trembling little
sheep.

In no time at all the shepherd had lifted it
from its hiding place and laid it across his
comforting shoulder. He hardly noticed the

long rough road on the way back, he was so
thankful that he had found his lost sheep.

When he got home he could not rest until he
had told his friends and neighbours all that had
happened.

"Rejoice with me," he said to them, "for I
have found my sheep which was lost."

3 The Sower

A farmer went out one morning to sow the new seed for next year's crop. The ground was prepared, the weather was good and he set off cheerfully for the day's work. Up and down the field he walked, scattering the seed this way and that.

Some of the seed slipped through his fingers on to the hard pathway which ran down the centre of the field; a flock of birds, following after him, swooped down and pecked it up, glad of the chance of a meal.

Some of it fell where only a thin layer of soil covered the rocky crust beneath; and some drifted away to the edge of the field and landed among the border of thorns and scrub growing there.

21

At last the sower's bag was empty, and so home he went. He was tired, but he felt satisfied with a job well done. The little brown seeds lay hidden in the earth just where they had fallen.

By the spring the seeds had sprouted and had pushed up young shoots, but the field had an oddly patchy look about it. The seeds that had

fallen on rocky ground had quickly sprouted in the thin soil; but when the sun came out, it scorched the unprotected roots and the tiny plants shrivelled and died.

The seeds which had fallen around the edge of the field had soon been smothered and choked by the fast-growing weeds and brambles. But the rest of the field was covered in the fresh green of young corn where the seeds had put down roots in the rich earth and had thrown up strong, healthy shoots.

When the corn was ready to harvest, the farmer took his sickle and cut it down. As he gathered it all in, he found that instead of the mere bagful of seeds that he had sown he now had a great pile of full ripe grains.

In spite of the fact that some of his labour was wasted effort, in the end the sower reaped the rewards of his hard work.

4 The Wheat and the Tares

It was night-time. Everyone in the farmhouse was fast asleep. The farmer and his servants were tired out. All day they had been labouring in the fields, sowing the new seed for next year's crops. Now the job was finished, and it was only a matter of time before the fresh plants would appear.

But the good farmer had an enemy, a man who hated him and wanted to harm him. This man had secretly spied on the farmer while he was at work. When he saw that the sowing was completed and that the household was in bed and fast asleep, he crept into the field and threw handfuls of weed seed amongst the seed for the crop. He then crept away.

Over the next few weeks the rain fell and the

sun shone, and the seeds began to sprout until the whole field was at last covered in pale green shoots. At first the good plants and the tares – which are a weed that grows among wheat – looked just the same, but one day a farm labourer noticed that some of the leaves were of different shape and a different shade of green.

He pointed this out to his fellow workers, and they all called the farm-owner to come and have a look.

"Sir," they said to him, "didn't you sow good seed in this field? Where did all these weeds come from?"

"An enemy must have done this," he answered sadly.

His men then asked, "Shall we go all over the field and pull up the weeds?"

The farmer thought about this suggestion for a moment. He looked closely at all the wheat shoots mixed up with the coarse weeds in the densely growing field. He realised that much of the crop would be destroyed if his servants trampled into the field at this stage. Sometimes it is better not to divide things up too quickly.

25

"No," he replied. "Right now it would be quite impossible to separate them one from the other without causing a great deal of damage. While trying to tear out the tares you would also, accidentally, uproot too much wheat. Let them all grow together until harvest-time. When the plants are full grown it will be quite obvious which are wheat and which are not. Then I shall tell the reapers to pull up all the weeds first and to tie them into bundles to be burned. After that they can gather in the wheat and put it safely in my barn. In this way I will be able to make sure that nothing that is good will be lost in the end."

5 The Hidden Treasure

One cold and frosty morning a poor labourer was ploughing a landowner's fields. It was heavy-going as he worked his way up and down the strip of land. Suddenly the plough-share stopped short as it struck against something particularly hard and unyielding under the soil.

"I expect that it's just a large lump of rock," the labourer grumbled wearily to himself. "How many I have moved already today! I've never known a field with so many stones in it. I wonder if I can shift this one?"

He let go of the plough handle and told the two oxen to stand still. The animals waited as he scraped away at the rough earth with his bare hands. After a little while he uncovered what appeared to be the edge of a large box.

This is too much for me to move by myself, he thought, and so he went back to ask for the farmer's help.

"Get back to your work, man," his employer answered impatiently. "Don't waste your time and my money with such things!"

But by now the man was curious to know if it *was* a box, and, if so, what was in it. So he fetched a spade, and, with a great deal of grunting and groaning, managed to dig the

obstruction out of the ground. He discovered that it was indeed a box – but no ordinary one. As he rubbed away the encrusted mud and dirt, elaborate designs began to appear on its surface.

When he finally uncovered the fastening and prized open the lid, the sight that met his eyes made him gasp. Inside, protected from the atmosphere and still brightly shining, were

richly decorated dishes and cups, knives and spoons with jewelled handles, sparkling chains and necklaces.

The man was overwhelmed by what he saw. After he had stared at the contents for some time, he let the lid fall back into place. "I must do some hard thinking," he said to himself. "This is a chance of a lifetime. If I take it back to the farmer, he will grab it from me and sell it. He refused to help me when I discovered it.

Why should I hand it over to him? And yet if I try to move it away now, someone will surely notice me. The best thing to do for the moment is nothing. I will cover the chest over again and continue with my ploughing."

During the next few days the neighbours were amazed to hear that the ploughman was selling up everything that he had. Not that he had much! But all that he had, he sold.

"Has he gone mad?" they asked each other. "He has lived here all his life. Where will he

go? What will he do?"

But the man knew exactly what he was doing. When he had gathered his cash together, he went to the landowner and asked if he could buy the field from him. The farmer was delighted to get rid of that poor stony piece of land for such a high offer. He, too, thought the man had gone crazy, but he greedily pocketed the money.

And so it was that the labourer took his chance and got the field, and, with it, the great treasure.

Sometimes we all have to sell or sacrifice things in order to gain our heart's desire.

6 The Parable of the Talents

A man once had to go away from home on a long journey. This meant leaving his three servants in charge of all his property.

"They are young," he said to himself, "but I think they are all trustworthy. I should like to retire soon and leave them to run my affairs. This will be a good chance to see how they each manage without me telling them what to do."

He thought it over, and decided to entrust a different amount of money to each servant according to his ability. So he called the three young men to him, and to the first he gave five 'talents', or bags of gold; to the second he gave two talents, and to the third and last, he gave just one. Then he set off on his journey.

The first servant took his five talents into the

town and by investing them wisely, doubled his money. The second servant used his two talents to buy some goods which he then sold at a profit. He also increased his share two-fold. But the third servant went outside and dug a deep hole. He took his one talent and hid it in the ground.

At last the master returned home. He summoned his three servants to him, one by one, and asked them to account for the money he had left them. The first servant produced his ten talents. "You gave me five, sir," he said, "but I took a chance and invested them, and now I can hand over ten."

"Well done, you good and faithful servant!"

said his master. "You have shown yourself well able to manage small sums of money. From now on I will trust you with much larger amounts. Let us drink to your promotion!"

Next the servant with the two talents came in. "Sir," he said, "I bought some goods with the two talents you gave me, and sold them at a profit. So I am pleased to be able to hand back four talents."

His master said to him, "Well done, you good and faithful servant! You too have shown what you are capable of. In future I shall give you more responsibility. Come and join us in a celebration drink!"

Then the servant with the one talent came in and said: "I know you are a stern master. I was afraid that I might lose your money, so I did the safest thing and hid it in the ground. Now I can give it back," and he produced his one talent.

His master was extremely annoyed.

"What a waste!" he said. "If you were too frightened of me to take a chance, at least you could have put my money in the bank where it would have earned some interest. Hiding it in

the ground is the most useless thing you could
have done. How could any good come of that?
You should have shown some courage as the
other two servants did, and made full use of
the talent given to you, instead of just burying
it away.''

If we inherit, or are given money or ability
(talent has had *both* meanings), it is essential to
use them. If we do not, they will become rusty
and useless; we will have failed to make the
best of what we have. Often this means taking
risks, but if we fail to have the courage to risk a
bit, we are in danger of losing everything.

7 The Wise and Foolish Bridesmaids

It was the day of the wedding. The ten
bridesmaids were waiting for the bridegroom
to come and collect them. He had arranged to
do so as soon as everything was ready for the
ceremony. That was the custom in that country.

The wedding was to take place in the evening,
and, instead of a posy of flowers, each brides-
maid would carry a lantern. It would make a
lovely sight – the ten girls filing along in
procession each with her little globe of light.

As they sat and waited, it began to get dark.
Their lamps burned steadily as the time passed.
Five of the girls had had the forethought to
bring an extra flask of oil. We have no idea how
long we shall have to wait, they had thought.
We must be prepared for our lamps to burn out.

The other five girls were flighty and foolish.
They were impatient to get on with the
festivities and they had not stopped to take
sensible precautions.

The hours went by and still there was no
sign of the bridegroom. It had been a long day,
and, one by one, the girls stopped chattering
excitedly to each other. At last they all fell
asleep.

It was midnight when they were suddenly
awakened by a voice outside, calling, ''The
bridegroom is coming. Come outside and meet
him.''

Springing to their feet, the bridesmaids
hastily brushed the sleep from their eyes and
the creases from their clothes.

Each picked up her lantern, but by now the

oil had almost burned through and the flame was low and feeble. In the dim light the five sensible girls carefully refilled their lanterns from their extra flasks of oil. The other five said to them, "Give us some of your oil; our lamps are beginning to go out."

"I'm afraid we can't do that," the wise ones answered. "There is not enough to go round. You will have to go out and see if you can buy some."

It seemed the only thing to do. So, with their lamps burning lower and lower, the five silly girls ran outside into the street in a frantic search for oil.

No sooner had they gone than the bridegroom appeared. The five girls with their lamps burning brightly went off with him to join the rest of the wedding-party. He led them into the house and shut the door.

Much later on, having found a fresh supply of oil and refilled their lamps, the other girls arrived. Light streamed from the windows of the house, and the shadows of the people inside passed backwards and forwards to the sounds of music and laughter.

Outside the five girls knocked on the closed door. "Sir, sir!" they called out. "We are here, let us in." But the bridegroom only shook his head and turned away. "I do not know who these people are," he said.

The girls went away, sadly reflecting that it pays to be prepared.

8 The Houses built on Rock and Sand

There were once two men who were left a lot
of money. "At last, we can fulfil our ambitions,"
they said to each other. We can have homes of
our own. We each have enough money to buy a
plot of land, bricks and mortar, timber, and
everything else needed to build a house."

The first one was a careful type of man; he
thought and planned for quite a long time
about what sort of house he would have and
where he would build it.

"The most important thing is the land on
which it is built," he said to himself. "My
house must have a firm foundation."

And so he went out and thoroughly explored
the surrounding countryside, all the time
looking for a place to give his house a solid

base. At last he found just what he wanted: a spacious and rocky plateau, well above any streams which might cause dampness. And there he built his house.

The other man had different ideas. He was in a great hurry to see his house finished; he wanted a beautiful house and garden. He found the prettiest site that he could; trees and bushes were sprouting out of the sandy soil, and a little stream flowed through from a nearby river. It was a perfect scene. And there he built his house.

Not long after the two men had finished their houses and moved in, violent winter storms

began. The winds blew at hurricane force; the rain poured down in torrents, and the rivers flooded over their banks.

The first house withstood all the strain and stress. It was built on rock and above any waters. When the storms passed it still stood firm and secure.

But the flood water seeped through the sandy soil and into the foundations of the other house. Alarming cracks soon appeared in the walls, and pieces of plaster fell off. Suddenly there was a tremendous crash as the whole building collapsed!

When the storms passed away from that spot, nothing remained there but a ruin.

9 Lazarus and the Rich Man

There was once an exceedingly rich man. His house was the largest and grandest in the city. His clothes were made of the finest purple cloth, and his servants prepared him food fit for a king. He held lavish parties for his rich relations, yet he never gave a thought to the poor and needy.

Outside the gates of the rich man's house lay a beggar-man called Lazarus. He had no home to go to. He had lived a wretched life without money, health or friends. Each time the rich man or his friends passed by, he raised a feeble hand in the hope that he might be thrown a few scraps of food. There he lay, little more than skin and bones, and the stray dogs came round and licked the unsightly sores that covered his body. But the rich man spared him hardly a glance.

Lazarus died, and the angels took him up into Heaven. Shortly afterwards, the rich man also died. He was taken down into Hell where he suffered terrible pain and torment. Far off in Heaven, he could see Abraham, Father of the Jewish people, with Lazarus by his side.

"Father Abraham," he cried out, "take pity on me. Tell Lazarus to dip his fingers in water and then send him down to cool my scorched tongue and burning throat. I am in agony from these flames."

But Abraham said, "Don't you remember, my
son, how during your lifetime, you had all the
good things while Lazarus had nothing but
bad? Now the positions are reversed. He is
comforted and happy; it is your turn to suffer.
And that is not all. There is a great gulf between
Heaven and Hell; no one can cross from one
side to the other."

The rich man understood then that nothing
could be done to relieve the suffering which he
had brought upon himself, but he thought
about his five brothers. They, too, lived in
luxury, caring little for anyone less fortunate
than themselves.

"I beg you, Father," he said, "send Lazarus to my father's house where my five brothers live. Tell him to warn them about what will happen if they do as I did. They, at least, can be spared this pain."

Abraham answered: "They have Moses and the prophets to warn them: let your brothers listen to them."

"That is not enough," cried the rich man. "But if someone were to come back from the dead to tell them, they would surely repent and live better lives."

But Abraham said: "If they will not heed the warnings of Moses and the prophets, then nothing will convince them. Even if someone were to rise from the dead, they still would not listen."

10 The Labourers in the Vineyard

The owner of a vineyard went out early one morning and saw that his grapes were ready for harvesting. They hung in great ripe clusters, their skins covered in a soft purple bloom. He looked at the cloudless sky, and called to his foreman.

"It is perfect weather for the harvest," he said to him. "You'll need help. I'll go at once to the market-place and hire some men."

So he went down the hillside to the town below. Although it was early in the day, the market-place was already busy. Everyone was up and about. Other local farmers had also come there to find help for their harvest, and farm labourers were gathered in groups hoping to be taken on for a day's employment. The owner of the vineyard went up to the nearest group and offered each man a silver coin, the going rate for a day's work. They all accepted and went off at once to get started.

At nine o'clock, when the harvesting was well under way, the owner saw that the crop was so heavy that he could do with some more help. So he went back to the market-place and engaged some more workers.

"Go to my vineyard," he said, "and I will pay you a fair wage."

Then at twelve o'clock and again at three o'clock, he did the same thing.

The weather changed during the day, and it looked as if a storm was brewing.

"We must get these grapes in before it rains," he said anxiously to his foreman. "It is unlikely that there is anyone left in the market-place, but I will go and see."

It was nearly five o'clock when he went back yet again to the town. The sun was beginning to sink behind gathering clouds and the air was much cooler. The market-place was empty except for a small group of men sitting idly under a tree. The owner recognised them as some of the workers he had seen there earlier in the day.

"Why are you wasting the whole day here doing nothing?" he asked.

"Nobody hired us," they answered. "We have given up hope of any work today."

"I need more men," he told them. "Go at once and start work in my vineyard."

When evening came, all the grapes had been safely gathered in. The baskets were full to overflowing with perfect fruit. The owner told his foremen, "Call the workers together, and pay them their wages, beginning with those I hired last, and ending with those I hired first."

The men who had started work at five o'clock were each paid a silver coin. When the men who were hired first came to be paid they thought they would get more, but they too were given a silver coin.

"This is all wrong," they said to each other. "We ought to get more money because we worked longer hours. We must go and complain about it."

So they took their money, and the man who was acting as spokesman for the rest said to the owner, "There are some men here who have been working for only one hour. We have put in a whole day's work, and when the sun was at its hottest, yet you have paid them the same as us.''

''Look, my friend,'' the owner answered him, ''you can't accuse me of cheating you. We agreed about the rate of pay from the outset. You thought a silver coin was a fair wage for the job. Take what you have been given and go home. If I choose to give the last group of workers as much as you, that is entirely my business. Aren't you feeling dissatisfied and jealous simply because I am being generous?''

It is always wrong to respond to someone else's generosity to others with our own resentment. It is a hard lesson to learn, and the story makes this clear by the difficulty we have in accepting that the first workers were not hard-done-by!

11 The Unmerciful Servant

There was once a king whose dominions stretched far and wide. Much of his time was spent travelling around his distant estates, and so he left his home affairs and the management of his money in the hands of his servants.

One day, when he was home after many months away, he decided that it was high time he checked up on his accounts. Almost as soon as he had opened the ledgers, he discovered that one of the servants had been borrowing his money and now owed him thousands of pounds.

The king called the man to him and demanded that he should repay his debt, but the servant replied that he had no possible means of doing so.

"In that case," said his master, "I shall seize

all your possessions and sell them off. I shall then sell you, your wife, and your children into slavery."

On hearing this, the servant fell on his knees and pleaded with him: "Be patient with me and I will pay you back every penny that I owe you."

The king's anger melted away and he relented. "Very well," he said. "I will let you off the debt altogether, and you can go free."

The servant left the room and, just outside, he met a fellow servant who owed him a few pounds. Grabbing the poor man by the throat

and almost choking him, he demanded his
money back.

The other servant fell on his knees and
begged him: "Be patient with me, and I will
repay it all."

But the hard-hearted servant refused his
request, and had him taken away and locked up
in prison until the money be repaid.

When the rest of the servants heard what
had happened they were outraged. They went
at once to the king and told him all about it.

Their master summoned the servant and said to him: "You villain! I took pity on you because you asked me to, and I let you off the whole of that enormous debt. You should have had mercy on your fellow servant, just as I had mercy on you."

Then the king ordered his officers to take the servant away and throw him into jail.

"Let him remain there and be punished until the debt is paid in full," he commanded.

Perhaps that servant in his prison cell came to see the truth that if men want mercy and forgiveness for themselves, they must offer them to other people first.

12 The Prodigal Son

There was once a man who had two sons. All their lives they had lived at home and worked on his land.

One day, the younger son went to his father and said, "Father, I know that all this property will eventually be divided between my brother and myself. We are old enough to manage our own lives. Can I have my share now? Why wait any longer?"

The father had misgivings about this idea, but he did as he was asked and gave each son his rightful portion. Within a few days, the younger son had sold his share, taken the money and left home.

He travelled abroad and set up home in another country in the centre of a town. It seemed a much more exciting place to live than the quiet farm he had known all his life. He bought some fine new clothes and soon began to make a new circle of friends.

Word quickly got around that here was a young man with money to spend, and his new friends were only too happy to help him spend it. They feasted and drank and held parties late into the night – all at his expense. None of them thought of working, but only of having a good time.

Before long, all the money was used up. Then the new friends no longer wanted to have anything to do with the young man. One by one they turned from him in disdain when he suggested that now it was *their* turn to help *him*. Penniless and friendless, he said sadly to himself, "There is nothing else for it. I must get a job."

But this was easier said than done. The harvest had failed that year and the country was in the grip of a famine. People had been thrown out of work, and there was not enough food to go round. The young man exchanged his fine clothes for something to eat; then, barefooted and in rags, he went from house to house, begging for work.

58

At last a rich farmer agreed to take him on, but only as a swineherd. In return for looking after the pigs, he was given board and lodging; but the lodging was only a corner of a barn, and the food was so meagre that in desperation he even tried eating the carob tree pods which the pigs fed on.

During the long lonely hours in the fields, the young man thought a great deal about his home. He remembered with remorse his father's unfailing kindness and generosity.

Even the servants had more than enough to eat and here am I almost starving to death! he thought to himself. The more he thought about it, the more he longed to go home.

He made up his mind to throw himself on his father's mercy. I shall go back, he decided, and say, "Father, I have done wrong. I am not worthy to be called your son. Make me one of your hired servants and let me work for you."

All this time the elder son had continued to work steadily on the farm. He seldom thought of his younger brother, but the absent son was never out of his father's thoughts. Each day he wondered where he was, and what he was doing. Every day he kept a look-out in the hope that at last he would see him returning.

One day when the father was waiting and watching, he saw in the distance a traveller coming slowly towards the house; he looked exhausted. While he was still a long way off, the father realised who it was.

"It is my son," he cried, and he ran out to meet him. "My son has come back to me." Flinging his arms round the dusty and ragged figure, he kissed him again and again.

The son said, "Father, I have done wrong. I am not worthy to be called your son."

But even as he spoke, his father was leading him back to the house, calling to the servants: "Quickly, quickly! Get my best robe and put it on my son. Put a ring on his hand and shoes on his feet. We must have a great feast. Kill a fatted calf that we may eat and be merry. For my son has come home. He was lost, and now he is found."

Meanwhile the elder son was out working in the fields. He had not seen his brother return. As he approached the house after his day's work, he was amazed to see bright lights in all the windows. He heard the sounds of music and laughter.

"Whatever is going on?" he asked one of the servants.

"Your brother is back," the servant informed him. "We have killed a fatted calf for a celebration feast as your father told us to do."

Then the elder brother was extremely angry. He refused to come into the house. Even when his father came out and begged him to come in, still he refused.

"I have lived at home all these years and worked very hard," he complained bitterly. "Not once have I ever disobeyed you. But you have never killed a fatted calf for *me*. You have never given *me* a ring. The minute my brother comes home, having spent all his money, you welcome him with open arms. He has been idle and wasteful, yet you give him the best of everything."

"My son," his father replied, "you are always with me and all that I have is yours. But it is right that we should be happy and thankful and celebrate today. It is as if your brother was dead, and is now alive. He was lost, and now he is found."

It is natural to feel some sympathy for the elder brother, but envy should have no place in a generous heart. He should not have been thinking about himself at all – but only of his brother's safe return home.